YANKEE BUGLE

U.S. ARMED FORCES

FML

FORMAL MEETING LOG

This book belongs to:

U.S. ARMED FORCES FORMAL MEETING LOG

ISBN-13: 978-0692539200 (Scroll Media)
ISBN-10: 0692539204

The Formal Meeting Log is produced by Yankee Bugle as a service of Scroll Media. Visit Yankee Bugle for more military-geared products and resources.

Yankee Bugle
www.yankeebugle.com

Scroll Media Company
www.scrollmedia.com

Scroll Bookstore
www.scrollbookstore.com

Printed in the United States of America.

ABOUT THIS LOG

Welcome to the U.S. Armed Forces Formal Meeting Log, designed to help every service member maximize military meetings by organizing planning, notes and takeaways from every formal briefing.

Once upon a time, few military members had ever seen a conference table, much less conducted a briefing around it. In the modern military, Americans are destroying terrorists 12,000 miles away from the comfort of air conditioned offices. While some lament this state of affairs, this is Patton's America where we focus more on helping the other poor bastard die for his country rather than us in ours. So instead of lamenting our PowerPoint Ranger status, let's make the most of it, at least until drones replace us entirely and someone activates Skynet.

THIS IS NOT A FIELD TOOL. But hey, it's your log now.

FOUO / PA / CLASSIFIED

This is not certified for use of For Official Use Only, Privacy Act or Classified information of any kind. This tool is for preparing for and tracking taskers to be reported upon and gained in the course of a formal military meeting. Please reserve sensitive information for the appropriate forms and disposable media that can be shredded upon use, as is directed by regulations.

ENTRY 001

DATE _____ **TIME** _____

LOC _____ **Rm.** _____

MTG TITLE / TOPIC _____

YOUR ROLE _____

ITEMS TO REPORT

▶ _____

▶ _____

▶ _____

▶ _____

▶ _____

Don't forget support documentation!

MISC DETAILS

_____

_____

_____

_____

_____

_____

_____

_____

_____

BRIEFING SLIDES

REQ? ☐ **WHEN DUE** _____ **SUBMIT?** ☐ **NO. SLIDES** _____

MTG NOTES

_____

_____

_____

_____

_____

_____

_____

_____

_____

_____

_____

_____

TASKERS & FOLLOW-UPS – Checkmark your Priorities

☐ _____

POC _____ DUE _____

☐ _____

POC _____ DUE _____

☐ _____

POC _____ DUE _____

☐ _____

POC _____ DUE _____

☐ _____

POC _____ DUE _____

ENTRY 002 DATE_____ TIME_____

LOC_____ Rm. _____

MTG TITLE / TOPIC _____

YOUR ROLE _____

ITEMS TO REPORT

▶ _____

▶ _____

▶ _____

▶ _____

▶ _____

Don't forget support documentation!

MISC DETAILS

_____

_____

_____

_____

_____

_____

_____

_____

_____

_____

BRIEFING SLIDES

REQ? ☐ WHEN DUE_____ SUBMIT?☐ NO. SLIDES ____

U.S. ARMED FORCES

MTG NOTES

_____

_____

_____

_____

_____

_____

_____

_____

_____

_____

_____

_____

TASKERS & FOLLOW-UPS - Checkmark your Priorities

☐ _____

POC _____ DUE _____

☐ _____

POC _____ DUE _____

☐ _____

POC _____ DUE _____

☐ _____

POC _____ DUE _____

☐ _____

POC _____ DUE _____

ENTRY 003 DATE_____ TIME_____

LOC_____ Rm. _____

MTG TITLE / TOPIC _____

YOUR ROLE _____

ITEMS TO REPORT

▶_____

▶_____

▶_____

▶_____

▶_____

Don't forget support documentation!

MISC DETAILS

_____

_____

_____

_____

_____

_____

_____

_____

_____

BRIEFING SLIDES

REQ? ☐ WHEN DUE_____ SUBMIT?☐ NO. SLIDES _____

U.S. ARMED FORCES

MTG NOTES

_____

_____

_____

_____

_____

_____

_____

_____

_____

_____

_____

_____

_____

TASKERS & FOLLOW-UPS – Checkmark your Priorities

☐ _____

   POC _____ DUE _____

☐ _____

   POC _____ DUE _____

☐ _____

   POC _____ DUE _____

☐ _____

   POC _____ DUE _____

☐ _____

   POC _____ DUE _____

ENTRY 004

DATE_____ TIME_____

LOC_____ Rm. _____

MTG TITLE / TOPIC _____

YOUR ROLE _____

ITEMS TO REPORT

▶ _____

▶ _____

▶ _____

▶ _____

▶ _____

Don't forget support documentation!

MISC DETAILS

_____

_____

_____

_____

_____

_____

_____

_____

_____

_____

BRIEFING SLIDES

REQ? ☐ WHEN DUE _____ SUBMIT? ☐ NO. SLIDES ____

MTG NOTES

_____

_____

_____

_____

_____

_____

_____

_____

_____

_____

_____

_____

TASKERS & FOLLOW-UPS – Checkmark your Priorities

☐ _____

   POC _____ DUE _____

☐ _____

   POC _____ DUE _____

☐ _____

   POC _____ DUE _____

☐ _____

   POC _____ DUE _____

☐ _____

   POC _____ DUE _____

ENTRY 005 DATE_____ TIME_____

LOC_____ Rm. _____

MTG TITLE / TOPIC _____

YOUR ROLE _____

ITEMS TO REPORT

▶_____

▶_____

▶_____

▶_____

▶_____

Don't forget support documentation!

MISC DETAILS

_____

_____

_____

_____

_____

_____

_____

_____

_____

_____

BRIEFING SLIDES

REQ? ☐ WHEN DUE_____ SUBMIT?☐ NO. SLIDES ____

MTG NOTES

_____

_____

_____

_____

_____

_____

_____

_____

_____

_____

_____

_____

_____

TASKERS & FOLLOW-UPS - Checkmark your Priorities

☐ _____

   POC _____ DUE _____

☐ _____

   POC _____ DUE _____

☐ _____

   POC _____ DUE _____

☐ _____

   POC _____ DUE _____

☐ _____

   POC _____ DUE _____

ENTRY 006 DATE_____ TIME_____

LOC_____ Rm. _____

MTG TITLE / TOPIC_____

YOUR ROLE   _____

ITEMS TO REPORT

▶_____

▶_____

▶_____

▶_____

▶_____

Don't forget support documentation!

MISC DETAILS

_____

_____

_____

_____

_____

_____

_____

_____

_____

BRIEFING SLIDES

REQ? ☐ **WHEN DUE**_____ **SUBMIT?** ☐ **NO. SLIDES** ____

MTG NOTES

_____
_____
_____
_____
_____
_____
_____
_____
_____
_____
_____
_____
_____

TASKERS & FOLLOW-UPS – Checkmark your Priorities

☐ _____

POC _____ DUE _____

☐ _____

POC _____ DUE _____

☐ _____

POC _____ DUE _____

☐ _____

POC _____ DUE _____

☐ _____

POC _____ DUE _____

MTG TITLE / TOPIC _____

YOUR ROLE _____

ITEMS TO REPORT

▶ _____

▶ _____

▶ _____

▶ _____

▶ _____

Don't forget support documentation!

MISC DETAILS

_____

_____

_____

_____

_____

_____

_____

_____

_____

_____

BRIEFING SLIDES

REQ? ☐ WHEN DUE_____ SUBMIT?☐ NO. SLIDES____

MTG NOTES

_____
_____
_____
_____
_____
_____
_____
_____
_____
_____
_____
_____
_____

TASKERS & FOLLOW-UPS – Checkmark your Priorities

☐ _____

POC _____ DUE _____

☐ _____

POC _____ DUE _____

☐ _____

POC _____ DUE _____

☐ _____

POC _____ DUE _____

☐ _____

POC _____ DUE _____

ENTRY 008 DATE_____ TIME_____

LOC_____ Rm._____

MTG TITLE / TOPIC _____

YOUR ROLE _____

ITEMS TO REPORT

▶ _____

▶ _____

▶ _____

▶ _____

▶ _____

Don't forget support documentation!

MISC DETAILS

_____

_____

_____

_____

_____

_____

_____

_____

_____

_____

BRIEFING SLIDES

REQ? ☐ WHEN DUE_____ SUBMIT? ☐ NO. SLIDES____

MTG NOTES

_____

_____

_____

_____

_____

_____

_____

_____

_____

_____

_____

_____

_____

TASKERS & FOLLOW-UPS - Checkmark your Priorities

☐ _____

POC _____ DUE _____

☐ _____

POC _____ DUE _____

☐ _____

POC _____ DUE _____

☐ _____

POC _____ DUE _____

☐ _____

POC _____ DUE _____

ENTRY 009

DATE_____ TIME_____

LOC_____ Rm. _____

MTG TITLE / TOPIC _____

YOUR ROLE _____

ITEMS TO REPORT

▶ _____

▶ _____

▶ _____

▶ _____

▶ _____

Don't forget support documentation!

MISC DETAILS

_____

_____

_____

_____

_____

_____

_____

_____

_____

BRIEFING SLIDES

REQ? ☐ WHEN DUE _____ SUBMIT? ☐ NO. SLIDES _____

MTG NOTES

_____

_____

_____

_____

_____

_____

_____

_____

_____

_____

_____

_____

_____

TASKERS & FOLLOW-UPS - Checkmark your Priorities

☐ _____

  POC _____ DUE _____

☐ _____

  POC _____ DUE _____

☐ _____

  POC _____ DUE _____

☐ _____

  POC _____ DUE _____

☐ _____

  POC _____ DUE _____

ENTRY 010 DATE_____ TIME_____

LOC_____ Rm. _____

MTG TITLE / TOPIC _____

YOUR ROLE _____

ITEMS TO REPORT

▶_____

▶_____

▶_____

▶_____

▶_____

Don't forget support documentation!

MISC DETAILS

_____

_____

_____

_____

_____

_____

_____

_____

_____

BRIEFING SLIDES

REQ? ☐ WHEN DUE _____ SUBMIT? ☐ NO. SLIDES ____

MTG NOTES

_____

_____

_____

_____

_____

_____

_____

_____

_____

_____

_____

_____

TASKERS & FOLLOW-UPS – Checkmark your Priorities

☐ _____

   POC _____ DUE _____

☐ _____

   POC _____ DUE _____

☐ _____

   POC _____ DUE _____

☐ _____

   POC _____ DUE _____

☐ _____

   POC _____ DUE _____

ENTRY 011 DATE_____ TIME_____

LOC_____ Rm. _____

MTG TITLE / TOPIC _____

YOUR ROLE _____

ITEMS TO REPORT

▶_____

▶_____

▶_____

▶_____

▶_____

Don't forget support documentation!

MISC DETAILS

_____

_____

_____

_____

_____

_____

_____

_____

_____

_____

BRIEFING SLIDES

REQ? ☐ WHEN DUE _____ SUBMIT? ☐ NO. SLIDES ____

MTG NOTES

_____

_____

_____

_____

_____

_____

_____

_____

_____

_____

_____

_____

TASKERS & FOLLOW-UPS – Checkmark your Priorities

☐ _____

   POC _____ DUE _____

☐ _____

   POC _____ DUE _____

☐ _____

   POC _____ DUE _____

☐ _____

   POC _____ DUE _____

☐ _____

   POC _____ DUE _____

DATE_____ TIME_____

LOC_____ Rm. _____

MTG TITLE / TOPIC _____

YOUR ROLE _____

ITEMS TO REPORT

▶ _____

▶ _____

▶ _____

▶ _____

▶ _____

Don't forget support documentation!

MISC DETAILS

_____

_____

_____

_____

_____

_____

_____

_____

_____

BRIEFING SLIDES

REQ? ☐ WHEN DUE_____ SUBMIT? ☐ NO. SLIDES _____

MTG NOTES

_____

_____

_____

_____

_____

_____

_____

_____

_____

_____

_____

_____

TASKERS & FOLLOW-UPS – Checkmark your Priorities

☐ _____

POC _____ DUE _____

☐ _____

POC _____ DUE _____

☐ _____

POC _____ DUE _____

☐ _____

POC _____ DUE _____

☐ _____

POC _____ DUE _____

ENTRY 013

DATE_____ TIME_____

LOC_____ Rm. _____

MTG TITLE / TOPIC _____

YOUR ROLE _____

ITEMS TO REPORT

▶_____

▶_____

▶_____

▶_____

▶_____

Don't forget support documentation!

MISC DETAILS

_____

_____

_____

_____

_____

_____

_____

_____

_____

BRIEFING SLIDES

REQ? ☐ WHEN DUE_____ SUBMIT? ☐ NO. SLIDES____

MTG NOTES

_____

_____

_____

_____

_____

_____

_____

_____

_____

_____

_____

_____

TASKERS & FOLLOW-UPS – Checkmark your Priorities

☐ _____

   POC _____ DUE _____

☐ _____

   POC _____ DUE _____

☐ _____

   POC _____ DUE _____

☐ _____

   POC _____ DUE _____

☐ _____

   POC _____ DUE _____

ENTRY 014

DATE_____ TIME_____

LOC_____ Rm. _____

MTG TITLE / TOPIC _____

YOUR ROLE _____

ITEMS TO REPORT

▶ _____

▶ _____

▶ _____

▶ _____

▶ _____

Don't forget support documentation!

MISC DETAILS

_____

_____

_____

_____

_____

_____

_____

_____

_____

BRIEFING SLIDES

REQ? ☐ WHEN DUE _____ SUBMIT? ☐ NO. SLIDES ____

MTG NOTES

_____

_____

_____

_____

_____

_____

_____

_____

_____

_____

_____

_____

TASKERS & FOLLOW-UPS – Checkmark your Priorities

☐ _____

POC _____ DUE _____

☐ _____

POC _____ DUE _____

☐ _____

POC _____ DUE _____

☐ _____

POC _____ DUE _____

☐ _____

POC _____ DUE _____

ENTRY 015 DATE_____ TIME_____

LOC_____ Rm. _____

MTG TITLE / TOPIC _____

YOUR ROLE _____

ITEMS TO REPORT

▶ _____

▶ _____

▶ _____

▶ _____

▶ _____

Don't forget support documentation!

MISC DETAILS

_____

_____

_____

_____

_____

_____

_____

_____

_____

BRIEFING SLIDES
REQ? ☐ WHEN DUE _____ SUBMIT? ☐ NO. SLIDES ____

MTG NOTES

_____
_____
_____
_____
_____
_____
_____
_____
_____
_____
_____
_____
_____
_____

TASKERS & FOLLOW-UPS – Checkmark your Priorities

☐ _____

    POC _____ DUE _____

☐ _____

    POC _____ DUE _____

☐ _____

    POC _____ DUE _____

☐ _____

    POC _____ DUE _____

☐ _____

    POC _____ DUE _____

ENTRY 016   DATE_____ TIME_____

LOC_____ Rm. _____

MTG TITLE / TOPIC _____

YOUR ROLE _____

ITEMS TO REPORT

▶_____

▶_____

▶_____

▶_____

▶_____

Don't forget support documentation!

MISC DETAILS

_____

_____

_____

_____

_____

_____

_____

_____

_____

BRIEFING SLIDES

REQ? ☐ WHEN DUE _____ SUBMIT? ☐ NO. SLIDES ____

MTG NOTES

_____

_____

_____

_____

_____

_____

_____

_____

_____

_____

_____

_____

TASKERS & FOLLOW-UPS – Checkmark your Priorities

☐ _____

POC _____ DUE _____

☐ _____

POC _____ DUE _____

☐ _____

POC _____ DUE _____

☐ _____

POC _____ DUE _____

☐ _____

POC _____ DUE _____

ENTRY 017

DATE_____ TIME_____

LOC_____ Rm. _____

MTG TITLE / TOPIC _____

YOUR ROLE _____

ITEMS TO REPORT

▶ _____

▶ _____

▶ _____

▶ _____

▶ _____

Don't forget support documentation!

MISC DETAILS

_____

_____

_____

_____

_____

_____

_____

_____

_____

BRIEFING SLIDES

REQ? ☐ WHEN DUE _____ SUBMIT? ☐ NO. SLIDES _____

MTG NOTES

_____

_____

_____

_____

_____

_____

_____

_____

_____

_____

_____

_____

TASKERS & FOLLOW-UPS – Checkmark your Priorities

☐ _____

   POC _____ DUE _____

☐ _____

   POC _____ DUE _____

☐ _____

   POC _____ DUE _____

☐ _____

   POC _____ DUE _____

☐ _____

   POC _____ DUE _____

ENTRY 018 DATE_____ TIME_____

LOC_____ Rm. _____

MTG TITLE / TOPIC _____

YOUR ROLE _____

ITEMS TO REPORT

▶_____

▶_____

▶_____

▶_____

▶_____

Don't forget support documentation!

MISC DETAILS

_____

_____

_____

_____

_____

_____

_____

_____

_____

BRIEFING SLIDES

REQ? ☐ WHEN DUE _____ SUBMIT? ☐ NO. SLIDES ____

MTG NOTES

_____

_____

_____

_____

_____

_____

_____

_____

_____

_____

_____

_____

TASKERS & FOLLOW-UPS – Checkmark your Priorities

☐ _____

POC _____ DUE _____

☐ _____

POC _____ DUE _____

☐ _____

POC _____ DUE _____

☐ _____

POC _____ DUE _____

☐ _____

POC _____ DUE _____

DATE_____ TIME_____

LOC_____ Rm. _____

MTG TITLE / TOPIC _____

YOUR ROLE _____

ITEMS TO REPORT

▶ _____

▶ _____

▶ _____

▶ _____

▶ _____

Don't forget support documentation!

MISC DETAILS

_____

_____

_____

_____

_____

_____

_____

_____

_____

BRIEFING SLIDES

REQ? ☐ WHEN DUE_____ SUBMIT? ☐ NO. SLIDES ____

MTG NOTES

_____

_____

_____

_____

_____

_____

_____

_____

_____

_____

_____

_____

_____

TASKERS & FOLLOW-UPS - Checkmark your Priorities

☐ _____

   POC _____ DUE _____

☐ _____

   POC _____ DUE _____

☐ _____

   POC _____ DUE _____

☐ _____

   POC _____ DUE _____

☐ _____

   POC _____ DUE _____

DATE_____ TIME_____

LOC_____ Rm. _____

MTG TITLE / TOPIC _____

YOUR ROLE _____

ITEMS TO REPORT

▶ _____

▶ _____

▶ _____

▶ _____

▶ _____

Don't forget support documentation!

MISC DETAILS

_____

_____

_____

_____

_____

_____

_____

_____

_____

BRIEFING SLIDES

REQ? ☐ WHEN DUE _____ SUBMIT? ☐ NO. SLIDES _____

MTG NOTES

_____

_____

_____

_____

_____

_____

_____

_____

_____

_____

_____

TASKERS & FOLLOW-UPS – Checkmark your Priorities

☐ _____

POC _____ DUE _____

☐ _____

POC _____ DUE _____

☐ _____

POC _____ DUE _____

☐ _____

POC _____ DUE _____

☐ _____

POC _____ DUE _____

ENTRY 021 DATE_____ TIME_____

LOC_____ Rm. _____

MTG TITLE / TOPIC _____

YOUR ROLE _____

ITEMS TO REPORT

▶ _____

▶ _____

▶ _____

▶ _____

▶ _____

Don't forget support documentation!

MISC DETAILS

_____

_____

_____

_____

_____

_____

_____

_____

_____

BRIEFING SLIDES

REQ? ☐ WHEN DUE _____ SUBMIT? ☐ NO. SLIDES _____

MTG NOTES

_____

_____

_____

_____

_____

_____

_____

_____

_____

_____

_____

TASKERS & FOLLOW-UPS – Checkmark your Priorities

☐ _____

   POC _____ DUE _____

☐ _____

   POC _____ DUE _____

☐ _____

   POC _____ DUE _____

☐ _____

   POC _____ DUE _____

☐ _____

   POC _____ DUE _____

DATE_____ TIME_____

LOC_____ Rm. _____

MTG TITLE / TOPIC _____

YOUR ROLE _____

ITEMS TO REPORT

▶_____

▶_____

▶_____

▶_____

▶_____

Don't forget support documentation!

MISC DETAILS

_____

_____

_____

_____

_____

_____

_____

_____

_____

BRIEFING SLIDES
REQ? ☐ WHEN DUE_____ SUBMIT? ☐ NO. SLIDES ____

MTG NOTES

_____

_____

_____

_____

_____

_____

_____

_____

_____

_____

_____

_____

_____

TASKERS & FOLLOW-UPS – Checkmark your Priorities

☐ _____

POC _____ DUE _____

☐ _____

POC _____ DUE _____

☐ _____

POC _____ DUE _____

☐ _____

POC _____ DUE _____

☐ _____

POC _____ DUE _____

ENTRY 023   DATE_____   TIME_____

LOC_____   Rm. _____

MTG TITLE / TOPIC _____

YOUR ROLE _____

ITEMS TO REPORT

▶_____

▶_____

▶_____

▶_____

▶_____

Don't forget support documentation!

MISC DETAILS

_____

_____

_____

_____

_____

_____

_____

_____

_____

BRIEFING SLIDES

REQ? ☐ WHEN DUE _____ SUBMIT?☐ NO. SLIDES _____

MTG NOTES

_____

_____

_____

_____

_____

_____

_____

_____

_____

_____

_____

_____

TASKERS & FOLLOW-UPS - Checkmark your Priorities

☐ _____

  POC _____ DUE _____

☐ _____

  POC _____ DUE _____

☐ _____

  POC _____ DUE _____

☐ _____

  POC _____ DUE _____

☐ _____

  POC _____ DUE _____

ENTRY 024 DATE_____ TIME_____

LOC_____ Rm. _____

MTG TITLE / TOPIC _____

YOUR ROLE _____

ITEMS TO REPORT

▶_____

▶_____

▶_____

▶_____

▶_____

Don't forget support documentation!

MISC DETAILS

_____

_____

_____

_____

_____

_____

_____

_____

_____

BRIEFING SLIDES

REQ? ☐ WHEN DUE_____ SUBMIT? ☐ NO. SLIDES ____

MTG NOTES

_____

_____

_____

_____

_____

_____

_____

_____

_____

_____

_____

_____

_____

TASKERS & FOLLOW-UPS – Checkmark your Priorities

☐ _____

   POC _____ DUE _____

☐ _____

   POC _____ DUE _____

☐ _____

   POC _____ DUE _____

☐ _____

   POC _____ DUE _____

☐ _____

   POC _____ DUE _____

ENTRY 025

DATE_____ TIME_____

LOC_____ Rm. _____

MTG TITLE / TOPIC _____

YOUR ROLE _____

ITEMS TO REPORT

▶ _____

▶ _____

▶ _____

▶ _____

▶ _____

Don't forget support documentation!

MISC DETAILS

_____

_____

_____

_____

_____

_____

_____

_____

_____

BRIEFING SLIDES

REQ? ☐ WHEN DUE _____ SUBMIT? ☐ NO. SLIDES ____

MTG NOTES

_____

_____

_____

_____

_____

_____

_____

_____

_____

_____

_____

_____

_____

TASKERS & FOLLOW-UPS – Checkmark your Priorities

☐ _____

   POC _____ DUE _____

☐ _____

   POC _____ DUE _____

☐ _____

   POC _____ DUE _____

☐ _____

   POC _____ DUE _____

☐ _____

   POC _____ DUE _____

ENTRY 026

DATE_____ TIME_____

LOC_____ Rm. _____

MTG TITLE / TOPIC _____

YOUR ROLE _____

ITEMS TO REPORT

▶_____

▶_____

▶_____

▶_____

▶_____

Don't forget support documentation!

MISC DETAILS

_____

_____

_____

_____

_____

_____

_____

_____

_____

BRIEFING SLIDES

REQ? ☐   WHEN DUE_____ SUBMIT?☐ NO. SLIDES ____

MTG NOTES

_____

_____

_____

_____

_____

_____

_____

_____

_____

_____

_____

TASKERS & FOLLOW-UPS – Checkmark your Priorities

☐ _____

POC _____ DUE _____

☐ _____

POC _____ DUE _____

☐ _____

POC _____ DUE _____

☐ _____

POC _____ DUE _____

☐ _____

POC _____ DUE _____

ENTRY 027 DATE_____ TIME_____

LOC_____ Rm. _____

MTG TITLE / TOPIC _____

YOUR ROLE _____

ITEMS TO REPORT

▶ _____

▶ _____

▶ _____

▶ _____

▶ _____

Don't forget support documentation!

MISC DETAILS

_____

_____

_____

_____

_____

_____

_____

_____

_____

BRIEFING SLIDES

REQ? ☐ WHEN DUE_____ SUBMIT? ☐ NO. SLIDES____

MTG NOTES

_____

_____

_____

_____

_____

_____

_____

_____

_____

_____

_____

_____

TASKERS & FOLLOW-UPS – Checkmark your Priorities

☐ _____

   POC _____ DUE _____

☐ _____

   POC _____ DUE _____

☐ _____

   POC _____ DUE _____

☐ _____

   POC _____ DUE _____

☐ _____

   POC _____ DUE _____

DATE_____ TIME_____

LOC_____ Rm. _____

MTG TITLE / TOPIC _____

YOUR ROLE _____

ITEMS TO REPORT

▶ _____

▶ _____

▶ _____

▶ _____

▶ _____

Don't forget support documentation!

MISC DETAILS

_____

_____

_____

_____

_____

_____

_____

_____

_____

_____

BRIEFING SLIDES

REQ? ☐ **WHEN DUE**_____ SUBMIT? ☐ **NO. SLIDES** ____

U.S. ARMED FORCES

MTG NOTES

_____

_____

_____

_____

_____

_____

_____

_____

_____

_____

_____

_____

TASKERS & FOLLOW-UPS - Checkmark your Priorities

☐ _____

POC _____ DUE _____

☐ _____

POC _____ DUE _____

☐ _____

POC _____ DUE _____

☐ _____

POC _____ DUE _____

☐ _____

POC _____ DUE _____

ENTRY 029 DATE_____ TIME_____

LOC_____ Rm. _____

MTG TITLE / TOPIC _____

YOUR ROLE _____

ITEMS TO REPORT

▶ _____

▶ _____

▶ _____

▶ _____

▶ _____

Don't forget support documentation!

MISC DETAILS

_____

_____

_____

_____

_____

_____

_____

_____

_____

BRIEFING SLIDES

REQ? ☐ WHEN DUE _____ SUBMIT? ☐ NO. SLIDES ____

MTG NOTES

_____

_____

_____

_____

_____

_____

_____

_____

_____

_____

_____

_____

TASKERS & FOLLOW-UPS – Checkmark your Priorities

☐ _____

   POC _____ DUE _____

☐ _____

   POC _____ DUE _____

☐ _____

   POC _____ DUE _____

☐ _____

   POC _____ DUE _____

☐ _____

   POC _____ DUE _____

ENTRY 030 DATE_____ TIME_____

LOC_____ Rm. _____

MTG TITLE / TOPIC _____

YOUR ROLE _____

ITEMS TO REPORT

▶ _____

▶ _____

▶ _____

▶ _____

▶ _____

Don't forget support documentation!

MISC DETAILS

_____

_____

_____

_____

_____

_____

_____

_____

_____

BRIEFING SLIDES

REQ? ☐ WHEN DUE _____ SUBMIT? ☐ NO. SLIDES ____

U.S. ARMED FORCES

MTG NOTES

_____

_____

_____

_____

_____

_____

_____

_____

_____

_____

_____

TASKERS & FOLLOW-UPS – Checkmark your Priorities

☐ _____

POC _____ DUE _____

☐ _____

POC _____ DUE _____

☐ _____

POC _____ DUE _____

☐ _____

POC _____ DUE _____

☐ _____

POC _____ DUE _____

ENTRY 031

DATE_____ TIME_____

LOC_____ Rm. _____

MTG TITLE / TOPIC _____

YOUR ROLE _____

ITEMS TO REPORT

▶ _____

▶ _____

▶ _____

▶ _____

▶ _____

Don't forget support documentation!

MISC DETAILS

_____

_____

_____

_____

_____

_____

_____

_____

_____

BRIEFING SLIDES

REQ? ☐ WHEN DUE_____ SUBMIT? ☐ NO. SLIDES____

MTG NOTES

_____

_____

_____

_____

_____

_____

_____

_____

_____

_____

_____

_____

TASKERS & FOLLOW-UPS – Checkmark your Priorities

☐ _____

POC _____ DUE _____

☐ _____

POC _____ DUE _____

☐ _____

POC _____ DUE _____

☐ _____

POC _____ DUE _____

☐ _____

POC _____ DUE _____

ENTRY 032

DATE_____ TIME_____

LOC_____ Rm._____

MTG TITLE / TOPIC _____

YOUR ROLE _____

ITEMS TO REPORT

▶_____

▶_____

▶_____

▶_____

▶_____

Don't forget support documentation!

MISC DETAILS

_____

_____

_____

_____

_____

_____

_____

_____

_____

BRIEFING SLIDES

REQ? ☐ WHEN DUE _____ SUBMIT? ☐ NO. SLIDES _____

U.S. ARMED FORCES

MTG NOTES

_____

_____

_____

_____

_____

_____

_____

_____

_____

_____

_____

TASKERS & FOLLOW-UPS – Checkmark your Priorities

☐ _____

   POC _____ DUE _____

☐ _____

   POC _____ DUE _____

☐ _____

   POC _____ DUE _____

☐ _____

   POC _____ DUE _____

☐ _____

   POC _____ DUE _____

DATE_____ TIME_____

LOC_____ Rm. _____

MTG TITLE / TOPIC _____

YOUR ROLE _____

ITEMS TO REPORT

▶ _____

▶ _____

▶ _____

▶ _____

▶ _____

Don't forget support documentation!

MISC DETAILS

_____

_____

_____

_____

_____

_____

_____

_____

_____

BRIEFING SLIDES

REQ? ☐   WHEN DUE _____   SUBMIT? ☐ NO. SLIDES ____

MTG NOTES

_____

_____

_____

_____

_____

_____

_____

_____

_____

_____

_____

_____

_____

TASKERS & FOLLOW-UPS – Checkmark your Priorities

☐ _____

POC _____ DUE _____

☐ _____

POC _____ DUE _____

☐ _____

POC _____ DUE _____

☐ _____

POC _____ DUE _____

☐ _____

POC _____ DUE _____

ENTRY 034

DATE_____ TIME_____

LOC_____ Rm. _____

MTG TITLE / TOPIC _____

YOUR ROLE _____

ITEMS TO REPORT

▶ _____

▶ _____

▶ _____

▶ _____

▶ _____

Don't forget support documentation!

MISC DETAILS

_____

_____

_____

_____

_____

_____

_____

_____

_____

BRIEFING SLIDES

REQ? ☐ WHEN DUE _____ SUBMIT? ☐ NO. SLIDES _____

U.S. ARMED FORCES

MTG NOTES

_____

_____

_____

_____

_____

_____

_____

_____

_____

_____

_____

_____

_____

TASKERS & FOLLOW-UPS – Checkmark your Priorities

☐ _____

   POC _____ DUE _____

☐ _____

   POC _____ DUE _____

☐ _____

   POC _____ DUE _____

☐ _____

   POC _____ DUE _____

☐ _____

   POC _____ DUE _____

ENTRY 035

DATE_____ TIME_____

LOC_____ Rm. _____

MTG TITLE / TOPIC _____

YOUR ROLE _____

ITEMS TO REPORT

▶ _____

▶ _____

▶ _____

▶ _____

▶ _____

Don't forget support documentation!

MISC DETAILS

_____

_____

_____

_____

_____

_____

_____

_____

_____

BRIEFING SLIDES

REQ? ☐ WHEN DUE _____ SUBMIT? ☐ NO. SLIDES ____

MTG NOTES

_____

_____

_____

_____

_____

_____

_____

_____

_____

_____

_____

_____

_____

TASKERS & FOLLOW-UPS – Checkmark your Priorities

☐ _____

POC _____ DUE _____

☐ _____

POC _____ DUE _____

☐ _____

POC _____ DUE _____

☐ _____

POC _____ DUE _____

☐ _____

POC _____ DUE _____

ENTRY 036 DATE_____ TIME_____

LOC_____ Rm. _____

MTG TITLE / TOPIC _____

YOUR ROLE _____

ITEMS TO REPORT

▶ _____

▶ _____

▶ _____

▶ _____

▶ _____

Don't forget support documentation!

MISC DETAILS

_____

_____

_____

_____

_____

_____

_____

_____

_____

BRIEFING SLIDES

REQ? ☐ WHEN DUE _____ SUBMIT? ☐ NO. SLIDES ____

MTG NOTES

_____

_____

_____

_____

_____

_____

_____

_____

_____

_____

_____

_____

TASKERS & FOLLOW-UPS – Checkmark your Priorities

☐ _____

POC _____ DUE _____

☐ _____

POC _____ DUE _____

☐ _____

POC _____ DUE _____

☐ _____

POC _____ DUE _____

☐ _____

POC _____ DUE _____

ENTRY 037

DATE_____ TIME_____

LOC_____ Rm. _____

MTG TITLE / TOPIC _____

YOUR ROLE _____

ITEMS TO REPORT

▶ _____

▶ _____

▶ _____

▶ _____

▶ _____

Don't forget support documentation!

MISC DETAILS

_____

_____

_____

_____

_____

_____

_____

_____

_____

_____

BRIEFING SLIDES

REQ? ☐ WHEN DUE _____ SUBMIT? ☐ NO. SLIDES ____

MTG NOTES

_____

_____

_____

_____

_____

_____

_____

_____

_____

_____

_____

_____

TASKERS & FOLLOW-UPS – Checkmark your Priorities

☐ _____

POC _____ DUE _____

☐ _____

POC _____ DUE _____

☐ _____

POC _____ DUE _____

☐ _____

POC _____ DUE _____

☐ _____

POC _____ DUE _____

ENTRY 038 DATE_____ TIME_____

LOC_____ Rm. _____

MTG TITLE / TOPIC _____

YOUR ROLE _____

ITEMS TO REPORT

▶_____

▶_____

▶_____

▶_____

▶_____

Don't forget support documentation!

MISC DETAILS

_____

_____

_____

_____

_____

_____

_____

_____

_____

_____

BRIEFING SLIDES

REQ? ☐ WHEN DUE _____ SUBMIT? ☐ NO. SLIDES ____

U.S. ARMED FORCES

MTG NOTES

_____

_____

_____

_____

_____

_____

_____

_____

_____

_____

TASKERS & FOLLOW-UPS - Checkmark your Priorities

☐ _____

POC _____ DUE _____

☐ _____

POC _____ DUE _____

☐ _____

POC _____ DUE _____

☐ _____

POC _____ DUE _____

☐ _____

POC _____ DUE _____

DATE_____ TIME_____

LOC_____ Rm. _____

MTG TITLE / TOPIC _____

YOUR ROLE _____

ITEMS TO REPORT

▶ _____

▶ _____

▶ _____

▶ _____

▶ _____

Don't forget support documentation!

MISC DETAILS

_____

_____

_____

_____

_____

_____

_____

_____

_____

BRIEFING SLIDES

REQ? ☐ **WHEN DUE**_____ SUBMIT? ☐ **NO. SLIDES** _____

MTG NOTES

_____

_____

_____

_____

_____

_____

_____

_____

_____

_____

_____

_____

_____

TASKERS & FOLLOW-UPS – Checkmark your Priorities

☐ _____

POC _____ DUE _____

☐ _____

POC _____ DUE _____

☐ _____

POC _____ DUE _____

☐ _____

POC _____ DUE _____

☐ _____

POC _____ DUE _____

ENTRY 040

DATE_____ TIME_____

LOC_____ Rm. _____

MTG TITLE / TOPIC _____

YOUR ROLE _____

ITEMS TO REPORT

▶_____

▶_____

▶_____

▶_____

▶_____

Don't forget support documentation!

MISC DETAILS

_____

_____

_____

_____

_____

_____

_____

_____

_____

BRIEFING SLIDES

REQ? ☐ WHEN DUE _____ SUBMIT? ☐ NO. SLIDES _____

U.S. ARMED FORCES

MTG NOTES

_____

_____

_____

_____

_____

_____

_____

_____

_____

_____

_____

_____

TASKERS & FOLLOW-UPS – Checkmark your Priorities

☐ _____

POC _____ DUE _____

☐ _____

POC _____ DUE _____

☐ _____

POC _____ DUE _____

☐ _____

POC _____ DUE _____

☐ _____

POC _____ DUE _____

ENTRY 041 DATE_____ TIME_____

LOC_____ Rm. _____

MTG TITLE / TOPIC _____

YOUR ROLE _____

ITEMS TO REPORT

▶ _____

▶ _____

▶ _____

▶ _____

▶ _____

Don't forget support documentation!

MISC DETAILS

_____

_____

_____

_____

_____

_____

_____

_____

_____

_____

BRIEFING SLIDES

REQ? ☐ WHEN DUE _____ SUBMIT? ☐ NO. SLIDES ____

U.S. ARMED FORCES

MTG NOTES

_____

_____

_____

_____

_____

_____

_____

_____

_____

_____

_____

_____

TASKERS & FOLLOW-UPS - Checkmark your Priorities

☐ _____

   POC _____ DUE _____

☐ _____

   POC _____ DUE _____

☐ _____

   POC _____ DUE _____

☐ _____

   POC _____ DUE _____

☐ _____

   POC _____ DUE _____

DATE_____ TIME_____

LOC_____ Rm. _____

MTG TITLE / TOPIC _____

YOUR ROLE _____

ITEMS TO REPORT

▶ _____

▶ _____

▶ _____

▶ _____

▶ _____

Don't forget support documentation!

MISC DETAILS

_____

_____

_____

_____

_____

_____

_____

_____

_____

BRIEFING SLIDES

REQ? ☐ WHEN DUE_____ SUBMIT? ☐ NO. SLIDES ____

MTG NOTES

_____

_____

_____

_____

_____

_____

_____

_____

_____

_____

_____

_____

_____

TASKERS & FOLLOW-UPS – Checkmark your Priorities

☐ _____

   POC _____ DUE _____

☐ _____

   POC _____ DUE _____

☐ _____

   POC _____ DUE _____

☐ _____

   POC _____ DUE _____

☐ _____

   POC _____ DUE _____

ENTRY 043

DATE_____ TIME_____

LOC_____ Rm. _____

MTG TITLE / TOPIC _____

YOUR ROLE _____

ITEMS TO REPORT

▶ _____

▶ _____

▶ _____

▶ _____

▶ _____

Don't forget support documentation!

MISC DETAILS

_____
_____
_____
_____
_____
_____
_____
_____
_____

BRIEFING SLIDES

REQ? ☐ WHEN DUE_____ SUBMIT? ☐ NO. SLIDES ____

MTG NOTES

_____

_____

_____

_____

_____

_____

_____

_____

_____

_____

_____

_____

_____

TASKERS & FOLLOW-UPS – Checkmark your Priorities

☐ _____

POC _____ DUE _____

☐ _____

POC _____ DUE _____

☐ _____

POC _____ DUE _____

☐ _____

POC _____ DUE _____

☐ _____

POC _____ DUE _____

DATE_____ TIME_____

LOC_____ Rm. _____

MTG TITLE / TOPIC _____

YOUR ROLE _____

ITEMS TO REPORT

▶ _____

▶ _____

▶ _____

▶ _____

▶ _____

Don't forget support documentation!

MISC DETAILS

_____

_____

_____

_____

_____

_____

_____

_____

_____

_____

BRIEFING SLIDES
REQ? ☐ **WHEN DUE** _____ SUBMIT?☐ NO. SLIDES ____

MTG NOTES

_____

_____

_____

_____

_____

_____

_____

_____

_____

_____

_____

_____

TASKERS & FOLLOW-UPS - Checkmark your Priorities

☐ _____

　POC _____ DUE _____

☐ _____

　POC _____ DUE _____

☐ _____

　POC _____ DUE _____

☐ _____

　POC _____ DUE _____

☐ _____

　POC _____ DUE _____

ENTRY 045

DATE_____ TIME_____

LOC_____ Rm. _____

MTG TITLE / TOPIC _____

YOUR ROLE _____

ITEMS TO REPORT

▶ _____

▶ _____

▶ _____

▶ _____

▶ _____

Don't forget support documentation!

MISC DETAILS

_____

_____

_____

_____

_____

_____

_____

_____

_____

BRIEFING SLIDES

REQ? ☐ WHEN DUE_____ SUBMIT? ☐ NO. SLIDES_____

MTG NOTES

_____

_____

_____

_____

_____

_____

_____

_____

_____

_____

_____

_____

TASKERS & FOLLOW-UPS – Checkmark your Priorities

☐ _____

　POC _____ DUE _____

☐ _____

　POC _____ DUE _____

☐ _____

　POC _____ DUE _____

☐ _____

　POC _____ DUE _____

☐ _____

　POC _____ DUE _____

LOC_____ Rm. _____

MTG TITLE / TOPIC _____

YOUR ROLE _____

ITEMS TO REPORT

▶_____

▶_____

▶_____

▶_____

▶_____

Don't forget support documentation!

MISC DETAILS

_____

_____

_____

_____

_____

_____

_____

_____

_____

_____

BRIEFING SLIDES
REQ? ☐ WHEN DUE_____ SUBMIT? ☐ NO. SLIDES ____

MTG NOTES

_____

_____

_____

_____

_____

_____

_____

_____

_____

_____

_____

_____

TASKERS & FOLLOW-UPS – Checkmark your Priorities

☐ _____

POC _____ DUE _____

☐ _____

POC _____ DUE _____

☐ _____

POC _____ DUE _____

☐ _____

POC _____ DUE _____

☐ _____

POC _____ DUE _____

ENTRY 047 DATE_____ TIME_____

LOC_____ Rm. _____

MTG TITLE / TOPIC _____

YOUR ROLE _____

ITEMS TO REPORT

▶_____

▶_____

▶_____

▶_____

▶_____

Don't forget support documentation!

MISC DETAILS

_____

_____

_____

_____

_____

_____

_____

_____

_____

BRIEFING SLIDES

REQ? ☐ WHEN DUE _____ SUBMIT? ☐ NO. SLIDES _____

MTG NOTES

_____
_____
_____
_____
_____
_____
_____
_____
_____
_____
_____
_____
_____

TASKERS & FOLLOW-UPS - Checkmark your Priorities

☐ _____

POC _____ DUE _____

☐ _____

POC _____ DUE _____

☐ _____

POC _____ DUE _____

☐ _____

POC _____ DUE _____

☐ _____

POC _____ DUE _____

ENTRY 048 DATE_____ TIME_____

LOC_____ Rm. _____

MTG TITLE / TOPIC _____

YOUR ROLE _____

ITEMS TO REPORT

▶_____

▶_____

▶_____

▶_____

▶_____

Don't forget support documentation!

MISC DETAILS

_____

_____

_____

_____

_____

_____

_____

_____

_____

_____

BRIEFING SLIDES

REQ? ☐ WHEN DUE_____ SUBMIT?☐ NO. SLIDES ____

MTG NOTES

_____

_____

_____

_____

_____

_____

_____

_____

_____

_____

_____

_____

TASKERS & FOLLOW-UPS – Checkmark your Priorities

☐ _____

   POC _____ DUE _____

☐ _____

   POC _____ DUE _____

☐ _____

   POC _____ DUE _____

☐ _____

   POC _____ DUE _____

☐ _____

   POC _____ DUE _____

ENTRY 049

DATE _____ **TIME** _____

LOC _____ **Rm.** _____

MTG TITLE / TOPIC _____

YOUR ROLE _____

ITEMS TO REPORT

▶ _____

▶ _____

▶ _____

▶ _____

▶ _____

Don't forget support documentation!

MISC DETAILS

_____

_____

_____

_____

_____

_____

_____

_____

_____

_____

BRIEFING SLIDES

REQ? ☐ **WHEN DUE** _____ **SUBMIT?** ☐ **NO. SLIDES** ____

U.S. ARMED FORCES

MTG NOTES

_____

_____

_____

_____

_____

_____

_____

_____

_____

_____

_____

_____

TASKERS & FOLLOW-UPS - Checkmark your Priorities

☐ _____

POC _____ DUE _____

☐ _____

POC _____ DUE _____

☐ _____

POC _____ DUE _____

☐ _____

POC _____ DUE _____

☐ _____

POC _____ DUE _____

ENTRY 050

DATE_____ TIME_____

LOC_____ Rm. _____

MTG TITLE / TOPIC _____

YOUR ROLE _____

ITEMS TO REPORT

▶ _____

▶ _____

▶ _____

▶ _____

▶ _____

Don't forget support documentation!

MISC DETAILS

_____

_____

_____

_____

_____

_____

_____

_____

_____

_____

BRIEFING SLIDES

REQ? ☐ WHEN DUE_____ SUBMIT?☐ NO. SLIDES ____

U.S. ARMED FORCES

MTG NOTES

_____

_____

_____

_____

_____

_____

_____

_____

_____

_____

_____

_____

TASKERS & FOLLOW-UPS - Checkmark your Priorities

☐ _____

POC _____ DUE _____

☐ _____

POC _____ DUE _____

☐ _____

POC _____ DUE _____

☐ _____

POC _____ DUE _____

☐ _____

POC _____ DUE _____

DATE_____ TIME_____

LOC_____ Rm. _____

MTG TITLE / TOPIC _____

YOUR ROLE _____

ITEMS TO REPORT

▶ _____

▶ _____

▶ _____

▶ _____

▶ _____

Don't forget support documentation!

MISC DETAILS

_____

_____

_____

_____

_____

_____

_____

_____

_____

BRIEFING SLIDES

REQ? ☐ **WHEN DUE** _____ **SUBMIT?** ☐ **NO. SLIDES** ____

MTG NOTES

_____

_____

_____

_____

_____

_____

_____

_____

_____

_____

_____

TASKERS & FOLLOW-UPS – Checkmark your Priorities

☐ _____

POC _____ DUE _____

☐ _____

POC _____ DUE _____

☐ _____

POC _____ DUE _____

☐ _____

POC _____ DUE _____

☐ _____

POC _____ DUE _____

FORMAL MEETING LOG

ENTRY 052 DATE_____ TIME_____

LOC_____ Rm. _____

MTG TITLE / TOPIC _____

YOUR ROLE _____

ITEMS TO REPORT

▶ _____

▶ _____

▶ _____

▶ _____

▶ _____

Don't forget support documentation!

MISC DETAILS

_____

_____

_____

_____

_____

_____

_____

_____

_____

BRIEFING SLIDES

REQ? ☐ WHEN DUE _____ SUBMIT? ☐ NO. SLIDES ____

MTG NOTES

_____

_____

_____

_____

_____

_____

_____

_____

_____

_____

_____

TASKERS & FOLLOW-UPS – Checkmark your Priorities

☐ _____

POC _____ DUE _____

☐ _____

POC _____ DUE _____

☐ _____

POC _____ DUE _____

☐ _____

POC _____ DUE _____

☐ _____

POC _____ DUE _____

ENTRY 053

DATE_____ TIME_____

LOC_____ Rm. _____

MTG TITLE / TOPIC _____

YOUR ROLE _____

ITEMS TO REPORT

▶ _____

▶ _____

▶ _____

▶ _____

▶ _____

Don't forget support documentation!

MISC DETAILS

_____

_____

_____

_____

_____

_____

_____

_____

_____

BRIEFING SLIDES

REQ? ☐ WHEN DUE _____ SUBMIT? ☐ NO. SLIDES _____

MTG NOTES

_____

_____

_____

_____

_____

_____

_____

_____

_____

_____

_____

_____

TASKERS & FOLLOW-UPS - Checkmark your Priorities

☐ _____

POC _____ DUE _____

☐ _____

POC _____ DUE _____

☐ _____

POC _____ DUE _____

☐ _____

POC _____ DUE _____

☐ _____

POC _____ DUE _____

ENTRY 054 DATE_____ TIME_____

LOC_____ Rm._____

MTG TITLE / TOPIC_____

YOUR ROLE _____

ITEMS TO REPORT

▶_____

▶_____

▶_____

▶_____

▶_____

Don't forget support documentation!

MISC DETAILS

_____

_____

_____

_____

_____

_____

_____

_____

_____

BRIEFING SLIDES

REQ? ☐ WHEN DUE_____ SUBMIT? ☐ NO. SLIDES____

U.S. ARMED FORCES

MTG NOTES

_____

_____

_____

_____

_____

_____

_____

_____

_____

_____

_____

_____

_____

TASKERS & FOLLOW-UPS – Checkmark your Priorities

☐ _____

   POC _____ DUE _____

☐ _____

   POC _____ DUE _____

☐ _____

   POC _____ DUE _____

☐ _____

   POC _____ DUE _____

☐ _____

   POC _____ DUE _____

ENTRY 055

DATE_____ TIME_____

LOC_____ Rm. _____

MTG TITLE / TOPIC _____

YOUR ROLE _____

ITEMS TO REPORT

▶ _____

▶ _____

▶ _____

▶ _____

▶ _____

Don't forget support documentation!

MISC DETAILS

_____

_____

_____

_____

_____

_____

_____

_____

_____

_____

BRIEFING SLIDES

REQ? ☐ WHEN DUE_____ SUBMIT?☐ NO. SLIDES _____

MTG NOTES

_____

_____

_____

_____

_____

_____

_____

_____

_____

_____

_____

_____

TASKERS & FOLLOW-UPS – Checkmark your Priorities

☐ _____

  POC _____ DUE _____

☐ _____

  POC _____ DUE _____

☐ _____

  POC _____ DUE _____

☐ _____

  POC _____ DUE _____

☐ _____

  POC _____ DUE _____

DATE_____ **TIME**_____

LOC_____ **Rm.** _____

MTG TITLE / TOPIC _____

YOUR ROLE _____

ITEMS TO REPORT

▶ _____

▶ _____

▶ _____

▶ _____

▶ _____

Don't forget support documentation!

MISC DETAILS

_____

_____

_____

_____

_____

_____

_____

_____

_____

BRIEFING SLIDES

REQ? ☐ **WHEN DUE**_____ **SUBMIT?** ☐ **NO. SLIDES** _____

MTG NOTES

_____
_____
_____
_____
_____
_____
_____
_____
_____
_____
_____
_____
_____

TASKERS & FOLLOW-UPS – Checkmark your Priorities

☐ _____

POC _____ DUE _____

☐ _____

POC _____ DUE _____

☐ _____

POC _____ DUE _____

☐ _____

POC _____ DUE _____

☐ _____

POC _____ DUE _____

FORMAL MEETING LOG

DATE_____ TIME_____

LOC_____ Rm. _____

MTG TITLE / TOPIC _____

YOUR ROLE _____

ITEMS TO REPORT

▶ _____

▶ _____

▶ _____

▶ _____

▶ _____

Don't forget support documentation!

MISC DETAILS

_____

_____

_____

_____

_____

_____

_____

_____

_____

BRIEFING SLIDES

REQ? ☐ WHEN DUE _____ SUBMIT? ☐ NO. SLIDES _____

MTG NOTES

_____

_____

_____

_____

_____

_____

_____

_____

_____

_____

_____

_____

TASKERS & FOLLOW-UPS – Checkmark your Priorities

☐ _____

   POC _____ DUE _____

☐ _____

   POC _____ DUE _____

☐ _____

   POC _____ DUE _____

☐ _____

   POC _____ DUE _____

☐ _____

   POC _____ DUE _____

ENTRY 058 DATE_____ TIME_____

LOC_____ Rm. _____

MTG TITLE / TOPIC _____

YOUR ROLE _____

ITEMS TO REPORT

▶ _____

▶ _____

▶ _____

▶ _____

▶ _____

Don't forget support documentation!

MISC DETAILS

_____

_____

_____

_____

_____

_____

_____

_____

_____

_____

BRIEFING SLIDES

REQ? ☐ **WHEN DUE** _____ **SUBMIT?** ☐ **NO. SLIDES** ____

MTG NOTES

_____

_____

_____

_____

_____

_____

_____

_____

_____

_____

_____

_____

_____

TASKERS & FOLLOW-UPS – Checkmark your Priorities

☐ _____

POC _____ DUE _____

☐ _____

POC _____ DUE _____

☐ _____

POC _____ DUE _____

☐ _____

POC _____ DUE _____

☐ _____

POC _____ DUE _____

ENTRY 059 DATE_____ TIME_____

LOC_____ Rm. _____

MTG TITLE / TOPIC _____

YOUR ROLE _____

ITEMS TO REPORT

▶ _____

▶ _____

▶ _____

▶ _____

▶ _____

Don't forget support documentation!

MISC DETAILS

_____

_____

_____

_____

_____

_____

_____

_____

_____

BRIEFING SLIDES

REQ? ☐ WHEN DUE_____ SUBMIT?☐ NO. SLIDES_____

MTG NOTES

_____
_____
_____
_____
_____
_____
_____
_____
_____
_____
_____
_____
_____

TASKERS & FOLLOW-UPS - Checkmark your Priorities

☐ _____

POC _____ DUE _____

☐ _____

POC _____ DUE _____

☐ _____

POC _____ DUE _____

☐ _____

POC _____ DUE _____

☐ _____

POC _____ DUE _____

ENTRY 060

DATE_____ TIME_____

LOC_____ Rm. _____

MTG TITLE / TOPIC _____

YOUR ROLE _____

ITEMS TO REPORT

▶ _____

▶ _____

▶ _____

▶ _____

▶ _____

Don't forget support documentation!

MISC DETAILS

_____

_____

_____

_____

_____

_____

_____

_____

_____

BRIEFING SLIDES

REQ? ☐ WHEN DUE _____ SUBMIT? ☐ NO. SLIDES ____

MTG NOTES

_____

_____

_____

_____

_____

_____

_____

_____

_____

_____

_____

_____

_____

TASKERS & FOLLOW-UPS - Checkmark your Priorities

☐ _____

  POC _____ DUE _____

☐ _____

  POC _____ DUE _____

☐ _____

  POC _____ DUE _____

☐ _____

  POC _____ DUE _____

☐ _____

  POC _____ DUE _____

ENTRY 061   DATE_____ TIME_____

LOC_____ Rm. _____

MTG TITLE / TOPIC _____

YOUR ROLE _____

ITEMS TO REPORT

▶ _____

▶ _____

▶ _____

▶ _____

▶ _____

Don't forget support documentation!

MISC DETAILS

_____

_____

_____

_____

_____

_____

_____

_____

_____

BRIEFING SLIDES

REQ? ☐ WHEN DUE _____ SUBMIT? ☐ NO. SLIDES ____

MTG NOTES

_____

_____

_____

_____

_____

_____

_____

_____

_____

_____

_____

TASKERS & FOLLOW-UPS – Checkmark your Priorities

☐ _____

POC _____ DUE _____

☐ _____

POC _____ DUE _____

☐ _____

POC _____ DUE _____

☐ _____

POC _____ DUE _____

☐ _____

POC _____ DUE _____

ENTRY 062 DATE_____ TIME_____

LOC_____ Rm. _____

MTG TITLE / TOPIC _____

YOUR ROLE _____

ITEMS TO REPORT

▶ _____

▶ _____

▶ _____

▶ _____

▶ _____

Don't forget support documentation!

MISC DETAILS

_____

_____

_____

_____

_____

_____

_____

_____

_____

BRIEFING SLIDES

REQ? ☐ WHEN DUE _____ SUBMIT? ☐ NO. SLIDES ____

MTG NOTES

_____

_____

_____

_____

_____

_____

_____

_____

_____

_____

_____

_____

_____

TASKERS & FOLLOW-UPS - Checkmark your Priorities

☐ _____

   POC _____ DUE _____

☐ _____

   POC _____ DUE _____

☐ _____

   POC _____ DUE _____

☐ _____

   POC _____ DUE _____

☐ _____

   POC _____ DUE _____

ENTRY 063

DATE_____ TIME_____

LOC_____ Rm. _____

MTG TITLE / TOPIC _____

YOUR ROLE _____

ITEMS TO REPORT

▶ _____

▶ _____

▶ _____

▶ _____

▶ _____

Don't forget support documentation!

MISC DETAILS

_____

_____

_____

_____

_____

_____

_____

_____

_____

BRIEFING SLIDES

REQ? ☐ WHEN DUE_____ SUBMIT? ☐ NO. SLIDES _____

MTG NOTES

_____

_____

_____

_____

_____

_____

_____

_____

_____

_____

_____

TASKERS & FOLLOW-UPS – Checkmark your Priorities

☐ _____

POC _____ DUE _____

☐ _____

POC _____ DUE _____

☐ _____

POC _____ DUE _____

☐ _____

POC _____ DUE _____

☐ _____

POC _____ DUE _____

ENTRY 064

DATE_____ TIME_____

LOC_____ Rm. _____

MTG TITLE / TOPIC _____

YOUR ROLE _____

ITEMS TO REPORT

▶ _____

▶ _____

▶ _____

▶ _____

▶ _____

Don't forget support documentation!

MISC DETAILS

_____

_____

_____

_____

_____

_____

_____

_____

_____

BRIEFING SLIDES

REQ? ☐ WHEN DUE _____ SUBMIT? ☐ NO. SLIDES ____

MTG NOTES

_____

_____

_____

_____

_____

_____

_____

_____

_____

_____

_____

_____

_____

TASKERS & FOLLOW-UPS – Checkmark your Priorities

☐ _____

   POC _____ DUE _____

☐ _____

   POC _____ DUE _____

☐ _____

   POC _____ DUE _____

☐ _____

   POC _____ DUE _____

☐ _____

   POC _____ DUE _____

DATE_____ TIME_____

LOC_____ Rm. _____

MTG TITLE / TOPIC _____

YOUR ROLE _____

ITEMS TO REPORT

▶ _____

▶ _____

▶ _____

▶ _____

▶ _____

Don't forget support documentation!

MISC DETAILS

_____

_____

_____

_____

_____

_____

_____

_____

_____

BRIEFING SLIDES

REQ? ☐ WHEN DUE_____ SUBMIT?☐ NO. SLIDES ____

U.S. ARMED FORCES

MTG NOTES

_____

_____

_____

_____

_____

_____

_____

_____

_____

_____

_____

_____

TASKERS & FOLLOW-UPS - Checkmark your Priorities

☐ _____

   POC _____ DUE _____

☐ _____

   POC _____ DUE _____

☐ _____

   POC _____ DUE _____

☐ _____

   POC _____ DUE _____

☐ _____

   POC _____ DUE _____

ENTRY 066 DATE_____ TIME_____

LOC_____ Rm. _____

MTG TITLE / TOPIC _____

YOUR ROLE _____

ITEMS TO REPORT

▶ _____

▶ _____

▶ _____

▶ _____

▶ _____

Don't forget support documentation!

MISC DETAILS

_____

_____

_____

_____

_____

_____

_____

_____

_____

BRIEFING SLIDES

REQ? ☐ WHEN DUE _____ SUBMIT? ☐ NO. SLIDES _____

U.S. ARMED FORCES

MTG NOTES

_____

_____

_____

_____

_____

_____

_____

_____

_____

_____

_____

_____

TASKERS & FOLLOW-UPS – Checkmark your Priorities

☐ _____

   POC _____ DUE _____

☐ _____

   POC _____ DUE _____

☐ _____

   POC _____ DUE _____

☐ _____

   POC _____ DUE _____

☐ _____

   POC _____ DUE _____

DATE_____ **TIME**_____

LOC_____ **Rm.** _____

MTG TITLE / TOPIC _____

YOUR ROLE _____

ITEMS TO REPORT

▶ _____

▶ _____

▶ _____

▶ _____

▶ _____

Don't forget support documentation!

MISC DETAILS

_____

_____

_____

_____

_____

_____

_____

_____

_____

_____

BRIEFING SLIDES

REQ? ☐ **WHEN DUE**_____ **SUBMIT?** ☐ **NO. SLIDES** _____

MTG NOTES

_____

_____

_____

_____

_____

_____

_____

_____

_____

_____

_____

_____

TASKERS & FOLLOW-UPS – Checkmark your Priorities

☐ _____

POC _____ DUE _____

☐ _____

POC _____ DUE _____

☐ _____

POC _____ DUE _____

☐ _____

POC _____ DUE _____

☐ _____

POC _____ DUE _____

DATE_____ TIME_____

LOC_____ Rm. _____

MTG TITLE / TOPIC _____

YOUR ROLE _____

ITEMS TO REPORT

▶_____

▶_____

▶_____

▶_____

▶_____

Don't forget support documentation!

MISC DETAILS

_____

_____

_____

_____

_____

_____

_____

_____

_____

_____

BRIEFING SLIDES

REQ? ☐ WHEN DUE_____ SUBMIT?☐ NO. SLIDES ____

MTG NOTES

_____

_____

_____

_____

_____

_____

_____

_____

_____

_____

_____

_____

_____

TASKERS & FOLLOW-UPS - Checkmark your Priorities

☐ _____

   POC _____ DUE _____

☐ _____

   POC _____ DUE _____

☐ _____

   POC _____ DUE _____

☐ _____

   POC _____ DUE _____

☐ _____

   POC _____ DUE _____

DATE_____ TIME_____

LOC_____ Rm. _____

MTG TITLE / TOPIC _____

YOUR ROLE _____

ITEMS TO REPORT

▶_____

▶_____

▶_____

▶_____

▶_____

Don't forget support documentation!

MISC DETAILS

_____

_____

_____

_____

_____

_____

_____

_____

_____

_____

BRIEFING SLIDES
REQ? ☐ **WHEN DUE**_____ SUBMIT?☐ NO. SLIDES ____

MTG NOTES

_____

_____

_____

_____

_____

_____

_____

_____

_____

_____

_____

_____

_____

TASKERS & FOLLOW-UPS – Checkmark your Priorities

☐ _____

POC _____ DUE _____

☐ _____

POC _____ DUE _____

☐ _____

POC _____ DUE _____

☐ _____

POC _____ DUE _____

☐ _____

POC _____ DUE _____

DATE_____ TIME_____

LOC_____ Rm. _____

MTG TITLE / TOPIC _____

YOUR ROLE _____

ITEMS TO REPORT

▶_____

▶_____

▶_____

▶_____

▶_____

Don't forget support documentation!

MISC DETAILS

_____

_____

_____

_____

_____

_____

_____

_____

_____

BRIEFING SLIDES

REQ? ☐ WHEN DUE_____ SUBMIT?☐ NO. SLIDES ____

MTG NOTES

_____

_____

_____

_____

_____

_____

_____

_____

_____

_____

_____

_____

TASKERS & FOLLOW-UPS – Checkmark your Priorities

☐ _____

POC _____ DUE _____

☐ _____

POC _____ DUE _____

☐ _____

POC _____ DUE _____

☐ _____

POC _____ DUE _____

☐ _____

POC _____ DUE _____

DATE_____ TIME_____

LOC_____ Rm. _____

MTG TITLE / TOPIC _____

YOUR ROLE _____

ITEMS TO REPORT

▶_____

▶_____

▶_____

▶_____

▶_____

Don't forget support documentation!

MISC DETAILS

_____

_____

_____

_____

_____

_____

_____

_____

_____

BRIEFING SLIDES

REQ? ☐ WHEN DUE_____ SUBMIT?☐ NO. SLIDES ____

U.S. ARMED FORCES

MTG NOTES

_____

_____

_____

_____

_____

_____

_____

_____

_____

_____

_____

_____

TASKERS & FOLLOW-UPS – Checkmark your Priorities

☐ _____

   POC _____ DUE _____

☐ _____

   POC _____ DUE _____

☐ _____

   POC _____ DUE _____

☐ _____

   POC _____ DUE _____

☐ _____

   POC _____ DUE _____

ENTRY 072 DATE_____ TIME_____

LOC_____ Rm. _____

MTG TITLE / TOPIC _____

YOUR ROLE _____

ITEMS TO REPORT

▶ _____

▶ _____

▶ _____

▶ _____

▶ _____

Don't forget support documentation!

MISC DETAILS

_____

_____

_____

_____

_____

_____

_____

_____

_____

BRIEFING SLIDES

REQ? ☐ WHEN DUE_____ SUBMIT? ☐ NO. SLIDES ____

MTG NOTES

_____
_____
_____
_____
_____
_____
_____
_____
_____
_____
_____
_____
_____

TASKERS & FOLLOW-UPS – Checkmark your Priorities

☐ _____

   POC _____ DUE _____

☐ _____

   POC _____ DUE _____

☐ _____

   POC _____ DUE _____

☐ _____

   POC _____ DUE _____

☐ _____

   POC _____ DUE _____

ENTRY 073

DATE_____ TIME_____

LOC_____ Rm. _____

MTG TITLE / TOPIC _____

YOUR ROLE _____

ITEMS TO REPORT

▶ _____

▶ _____

▶ _____

▶ _____

▶ _____

Don't forget support documentation!

MISC DETAILS

_____

_____

_____

_____

_____

_____

_____

_____

_____

BRIEFING SLIDES

REQ? ☐ WHEN DUE_____ SUBMIT? ☐ NO. SLIDES ____

MTG NOTES

_____

_____

_____

_____

_____

_____

_____

_____

_____

_____

_____

_____

_____

TASKERS & FOLLOW-UPS - Checkmark your Priorities

☐ _____

POC _____ DUE _____

☐ _____

POC _____ DUE _____

☐ _____

POC _____ DUE _____

☐ _____

POC _____ DUE _____

☐ _____

POC _____ DUE _____

ENTRY 074

DATE_____ TIME_____

LOC_____ Rm. _____

MTG TITLE / TOPIC _____

YOUR ROLE _____

ITEMS TO REPORT

▶ _____

▶ _____

▶ _____

▶ _____

▶ _____

Don't forget support documentation!

MISC DETAILS

_____

_____

_____

_____

_____

_____

_____

_____

_____

_____

BRIEFING SLIDES

REQ? ☐ WHEN DUE _____ SUBMIT?☐ NO. SLIDES _____

MTG NOTES

_____

_____

_____

_____

_____

_____

_____

_____

_____

_____

_____

_____

TASKERS & FOLLOW-UPS – Checkmark your Priorities

☐ _____

POC _____ DUE _____

☐ _____

POC _____ DUE _____

☐ _____

POC _____ DUE _____

☐ _____

POC _____ DUE _____

☐ _____

POC _____ DUE _____

DATE_____ TIME_____

LOC_____ Rm. _____

MTG TITLE / TOPIC _____

YOUR ROLE _____

ITEMS TO REPORT

▶ _____

▶ _____

▶ _____

▶ _____

▶ _____

Don't forget support documentation!

MISC DETAILS

_____

_____

_____

_____

_____

_____

_____

_____

_____

BRIEFING SLIDES

REQ? ☐ WHEN DUE_____ SUBMIT? ☐ NO. SLIDES _____

MTG NOTES

_____
_____
_____
_____
_____
_____
_____
_____
_____
_____
_____
_____
_____

TASKERS & FOLLOW-UPS – Checkmark your Priorities

☐ _____

POC _____ DUE _____

☐ _____

POC _____ DUE _____

☐ _____

POC _____ DUE _____

☐ _____

POC _____ DUE _____

☐ _____

POC _____ DUE _____

DATE_____ TIME_____

LOC_____ Rm. _____

MTG TITLE / TOPIC _____

YOUR ROLE _____

ITEMS TO REPORT

▶ _____

▶ _____

▶ _____

▶ _____

▶ _____

Don't forget support documentation!

MISC DETAILS

_____

_____

_____

_____

_____

_____

_____

_____

_____

BRIEFING SLIDES

REQ? ☐ WHEN DUE_____ SUBMIT? ☐ NO. SLIDES ____

MTG NOTES

_____

_____

_____

_____

_____

_____

_____

_____

_____

_____

_____

_____

_____

TASKERS & FOLLOW-UPS – Checkmark your Priorities

☐ _____

POC _____ DUE _____

☐ _____

POC _____ DUE _____

☐ _____

POC _____ DUE _____

☐ _____

POC _____ DUE _____

☐ _____

POC _____ DUE _____

DATE_____ TIME_____

LOC_____ Rm. _____

MTG TITLE / TOPIC _____

YOUR ROLE _____

ITEMS TO REPORT

▶_____

▶_____

▶_____

▶_____

▶_____

Don't forget support documentation!

MISC DETAILS

_____

_____

_____

_____

_____

_____

_____

_____

_____

BRIEFING SLIDES

REQ? ☐ WHEN DUE_____ SUBMIT?☐ NO. SLIDES ____

MTG NOTES

_____

_____

_____

_____

_____

_____

_____

_____

_____

_____

_____

_____

TASKERS & FOLLOW-UPS – Checkmark your Priorities

☐ _____

POC _____ DUE _____

☐ _____

POC _____ DUE _____

☐ _____

POC _____ DUE _____

☐ _____

POC _____ DUE _____

☐ _____

POC _____ DUE _____

ENTRY 078 DATE_____ TIME_____

LOC_____ Rm. _____

MTG TITLE / TOPIC _____

YOUR ROLE _____

ITEMS TO REPORT

▶ _____

▶ _____

▶ _____

▶ _____

▶ _____

Don't forget support documentation!

MISC DETAILS

_____

_____

_____

_____

_____

_____

_____

_____

_____

BRIEFING SLIDES

REQ? ☐ WHEN DUE _____ SUBMIT? ☐ NO. SLIDES ____

MTG NOTES

_____
_____
_____
_____
_____
_____
_____
_____
_____
_____
_____
_____
_____
_____

TASKERS & FOLLOW-UPS – Checkmark your Priorities

☐ _____

POC _____ DUE _____

☐ _____

POC _____ DUE _____

☐ _____

POC _____ DUE _____

☐ _____

POC _____ DUE _____

☐ _____

POC _____ DUE _____

DATE_____ TIME_____

LOC_____ Rm. _____

MTG TITLE / TOPIC _____

YOUR ROLE _____

ITEMS TO REPORT

▶_____

▶_____

▶_____

▶_____

▶_____

Don't forget support documentation!

MISC DETAILS

_____

_____

_____

_____

_____

_____

_____

_____

_____

BRIEFING SLIDES

REQ? ☐ WHEN DUE_____ SUBMIT?☐ NO. SLIDES ____

U.S. ARMED FORCES

MTG NOTES

_____
_____
_____
_____
_____
_____
_____
_____
_____
_____
_____
_____
_____

TASKERS & FOLLOW-UPS – Checkmark your Priorities

☐ _____

POC _____ DUE _____

☐ _____

POC _____ DUE _____

☐ _____

POC _____ DUE _____

☐ _____

POC _____ DUE _____

☐ _____

POC _____ DUE _____

DATE_____ TIME_____

LOC_____ Rm._____

MTG TITLE / TOPIC_____

YOUR ROLE_____

ITEMS TO REPORT

▶_____

▶_____

▶_____

▶_____

▶_____

Don't forget support documentation!

MISC DETAILS

_____

_____

_____

_____

_____

_____

_____

_____

_____

_____

BRIEFING SLIDES

REQ? ☐ WHEN DUE_____ SUBMIT? ☐ NO. SLIDES_____

MTG NOTES

_____

_____

_____

_____

_____

_____

_____

_____

_____

_____

_____

_____

TASKERS & FOLLOW-UPS – Checkmark your Priorities

☐ _____

POC _____ DUE _____

☐ _____

POC _____ DUE _____

☐ _____

POC _____ DUE _____

☐ _____

POC _____ DUE _____

☐ _____

POC _____ DUE _____

ENTRY 081 DATE_____ TIME_____

LOC_____ Rm. _____

MTG TITLE / TOPIC _____

YOUR ROLE _____

ITEMS TO REPORT

▶ _____

▶ _____

▶ _____

▶ _____

▶ _____

Don't forget support documentation!

MISC DETAILS

_____

_____

_____

_____

_____

_____

_____

_____

_____

_____

BRIEFING SLIDES

REQ? ☐ WHEN DUE _____ SUBMIT? ☐ NO. SLIDES _____

MTG NOTES

_____

_____

_____

_____

_____

_____

_____

_____

_____

_____

_____

_____

_____

TASKERS & FOLLOW-UPS – Checkmark your Priorities

☐ _____

POC _____ DUE _____

☐ _____

POC _____ DUE _____

☐ _____

POC _____ DUE _____

☐ _____

POC _____ DUE _____

☐ _____

POC _____ DUE _____

ENTRY 082

DATE_____ TIME_____

LOC_____ Rm. _____

MTG TITLE / TOPIC _____

YOUR ROLE _____

ITEMS TO REPORT

▶_____

▶_____

▶_____

▶_____

▶_____

Don't forget support documentation!

MISC DETAILS

_____

_____

_____

_____

_____

_____

_____

_____

_____

_____

BRIEFING SLIDES

REQ? ☐ WHEN DUE _____ SUBMIT? ☐ NO. SLIDES _____

U.S. ARMED FORCES

MTG NOTES

_____

_____

_____

_____

_____

_____

_____

_____

_____

_____

_____

_____

_____

TASKERS & FOLLOW-UPS – Checkmark your Priorities

☐ _____

POC _____ DUE _____

☐ _____

POC _____ DUE _____

☐ _____

POC _____ DUE _____

☐ _____

POC _____ DUE _____

☐ _____

POC _____ DUE _____

ENTRY 083

DATE_____ TIME_____

LOC_____ Rm. _____

MTG TITLE / TOPIC _____

YOUR ROLE _____

ITEMS TO REPORT

▶ _____

▶ _____

▶ _____

▶ _____

▶ _____

Don't forget support documentation!

MISC DETAILS

_____

_____

_____

_____

_____

_____

_____

_____

_____

_____

BRIEFING SLIDES

REQ? ☐ WHEN DUE _____ SUBMIT? ☐ NO. SLIDES _____

MTG NOTES

_____

_____

_____

_____

_____

_____

_____

_____

_____

_____

_____

_____

TASKERS & FOLLOW-UPS – Checkmark your Priorities

☐ _____

POC _____ DUE _____

☐ _____

POC _____ DUE _____

☐ _____

POC _____ DUE _____

☐ _____

POC _____ DUE _____

☐ _____

POC _____ DUE _____

MTG TITLE / TOPIC _____

YOUR ROLE _____

ITEMS TO REPORT

▶ _____

▶ _____

▶ _____

▶ _____

▶ _____

Don't forget support documentation!

MISC DETAILS

_____

_____

_____

_____

_____

_____

_____

_____

_____

BRIEFING SLIDES

REQ? ☐ WHEN DUE _____ SUBMIT? ☐ NO. SLIDES _____

MTG NOTES

_____

_____

_____

_____

_____

_____

_____

_____

_____

_____

_____

_____

_____

TASKERS & FOLLOW-UPS – Checkmark your Priorities

☐ _____

POC _____ DUE _____

☐ _____

POC _____ DUE _____

☐ _____

POC _____ DUE _____

☐ _____

POC _____ DUE _____

☐ _____

POC _____ DUE _____

DATE_____ TIME_____

LOC_____ Rm. _____

MTG TITLE / TOPIC _____

YOUR ROLE _____

ITEMS TO REPORT

▶ _____

▶ _____

▶ _____

▶ _____

▶ _____

Don't forget support documentation!

MISC DETAILS

_____

_____

_____

_____

_____

_____

_____

_____

_____

BRIEFING SLIDES

REQ? ☐ **WHEN DUE** _____ **SUBMIT?** ☐ **NO. SLIDES** ____

MTG NOTES

_____

_____

_____

_____

_____

_____

_____

_____

_____

_____

_____

_____

_____

TASKERS & FOLLOW-UPS – Checkmark your Priorities

☐ _____

  POC _____ DUE _____

☐ _____

  POC _____ DUE _____

☐ _____

  POC _____ DUE _____

☐ _____

  POC _____ DUE _____

☐ _____

  POC _____ DUE _____

ENTRY 086

DATE_____ TIME_____

LOC_____ Rm. _____

MTG TITLE / TOPIC_____

YOUR ROLE_____

ITEMS TO REPORT

▶_____

▶_____

▶_____

▶_____

▶_____

Don't forget support documentation!

MISC DETAILS

_____

_____

_____

_____

_____

_____

_____

_____

_____

BRIEFING SLIDES

REQ? ☐ WHEN DUE_____ SUBMIT?☐ NO. SLIDES _____

MTG NOTES

_____

_____

_____

_____

_____

_____

_____

_____

_____

_____

_____

_____

_____

TASKERS & FOLLOW-UPS - Checkmark your Priorities

☐ _____

POC _____ DUE _____

☐ _____

POC _____ DUE _____

☐ _____

POC _____ DUE _____

☐ _____

POC _____ DUE _____

☐ _____

POC _____ DUE _____

ENTRY 087   DATE_____ TIME_____

LOC_____ Rm. _____

MTG TITLE / TOPIC _____

YOUR ROLE _____

ITEMS TO REPORT

▶ _____

▶ _____

▶ _____

▶ _____

▶ _____

Don't forget support documentation!

MISC DETAILS

_____

_____

_____

_____

_____

_____

_____

_____

_____

BRIEFING SLIDES

REQ? ☐ WHEN DUE_____ SUBMIT? ☐ NO. SLIDES ____

MTG NOTES

_____

_____

_____

_____

_____

_____

_____

_____

_____

_____

_____

_____

_____

TASKERS & FOLLOW-UPS – Checkmark your Priorities

☐ _____

POC _____ DUE _____

☐ _____

POC _____ DUE _____

☐ _____

POC _____ DUE _____

☐ _____

POC _____ DUE _____

☐ _____

POC _____ DUE _____

DATE_____ TIME_____

LOC_____ Rm. _____

MTG TITLE / TOPIC _____

YOUR ROLE _____

ITEMS TO REPORT

▶ _____

▶ _____

▶ _____

▶ _____

▶ _____

Don't forget support documentation!

MISC DETAILS

_____

_____

_____

_____

_____

_____

_____

_____

_____

BRIEFING SLIDES

REQ? ☐ WHEN DUE_____ SUBMIT? ☐ NO. SLIDES _____

U.S. ARMED FORCES

MTG NOTES

_____

_____

_____

_____

_____

_____

_____

_____

_____

_____

_____

_____

_____

TASKERS & FOLLOW-UPS – Checkmark your Priorities

☐ _____

   POC _____ DUE _____

☐ _____

   POC _____ DUE _____

☐ _____

   POC _____ DUE _____

☐ _____

   POC _____ DUE _____

☐ _____

   POC _____ DUE _____

ENTRY 089

DATE_____ TIME_____

LOC_____ Rm. _____

MTG TITLE / TOPIC_____

YOUR ROLE   _____

ITEMS TO REPORT

▶ _____

▶ _____

▶ _____

▶ _____

▶ _____

Don't forget support documentation!

MISC DETAILS

_____

_____

_____

_____

_____

_____

_____

_____

_____

BRIEFING SLIDES

REQ? ☐ WHEN DUE _____ SUBMIT?☐ NO. SLIDES ____

MTG NOTES

_____

_____

_____

_____

_____

_____

_____

_____

_____

_____

_____

_____

TASKERS & FOLLOW-UPS – Checkmark your Priorities

☐ _____

POC _____ DUE _____

☐ _____

POC _____ DUE _____

☐ _____

POC _____ DUE _____

☐ _____

POC _____ DUE _____

☐ _____

POC _____ DUE _____

ENTRY 090

DATE_____ TIME_____

LOC_____ Rm. _____

MTG TITLE / TOPIC _____

YOUR ROLE _____

ITEMS TO REPORT

▶ _____

▶ _____

▶ _____

▶ _____

▶ _____

Don't forget support documentation!

MISC DETAILS

_____

_____

_____

_____

_____

_____

_____

_____

_____

BRIEFING SLIDES

REQ? ☐ WHEN DUE _____ SUBMIT? ☐ NO. SLIDES _____

MTG NOTES

_____

_____

_____

_____

_____

_____

_____

_____

_____

_____

_____

_____

_____

TASKERS & FOLLOW-UPS – Checkmark your Priorities

☐ _____

   POC _____ DUE _____

☐ _____

   POC _____ DUE _____

☐ _____

   POC _____ DUE _____

☐ _____

   POC _____ DUE _____

☐ _____

   POC _____ DUE _____

DATE_____ TIME_____

LOC_____ Rm. _____

MTG TITLE / TOPIC_____

YOUR ROLE_____

ITEMS TO REPORT

▶ _____

▶ _____

▶ _____

▶ _____

▶ _____

Don't forget support documentation!

MISC DETAILS

_____

_____

_____

_____

_____

_____

_____

_____

_____

BRIEFING SLIDES

REQ? ☐ WHEN DUE_____ SUBMIT? ☐ NO. SLIDES _____

U.S. ARMED FORCES

MTG NOTES

_____

_____

_____

_____

_____

_____

_____

_____

_____

_____

_____

_____

_____

TASKERS & FOLLOW-UPS – Checkmark your Priorities

☐ _____

   POC _____ DUE _____

☐ _____

   POC _____ DUE _____

☐ _____

   POC _____ DUE _____

☐ _____

   POC _____ DUE _____

☐ _____

   POC _____ DUE _____

ENTRY 092

DATE _____ TIME _____

LOC _____ Rm. _____

MTG TITLE / TOPIC _____

YOUR ROLE _____

ITEMS TO REPORT

▶ _____

▶ _____

▶ _____

▶ _____

▶ _____

Don't forget support documentation!

MISC DETAILS

_____

_____

_____

_____

_____

_____

_____

_____

_____

BRIEFING SLIDES

REQ? ☐ WHEN DUE _____ SUBMIT? ☐ NO. SLIDES _____

MTG NOTES

_____

_____

_____

_____

_____

_____

_____

_____

_____

_____

_____

_____

TASKERS & FOLLOW-UPS - Checkmark your Priorities

☐ _____

   POC _____ DUE _____

☐ _____

   POC _____ DUE _____

☐ _____

   POC _____ DUE _____

☐ _____

   POC _____ DUE _____

☐ _____

   POC _____ DUE _____

ENTRY 093

DATE_____ TIME_____

LOC_____ Rm. _____

MTG TITLE / TOPIC _____

YOUR ROLE _____

ITEMS TO REPORT

▶_____

▶_____

▶_____

▶_____

▶_____

Don't forget support documentation!

MISC DETAILS

_____

_____

_____

_____

_____

_____

_____

_____

_____

_____

BRIEFING SLIDES

REQ? ☐ WHEN DUE_____ SUBMIT? ☐ NO. SLIDES ____

MTG NOTES

_____

_____

_____

_____

_____

_____

_____

_____

_____

_____

_____

_____

TASKERS & FOLLOW-UPS - Checkmark your Priorities

☐ _____

POC _____ DUE _____

☐ _____

POC _____ DUE _____

☐ _____

POC _____ DUE _____

☐ _____

POC _____ DUE _____

☐ _____

POC _____ DUE _____

ENTRY 094

DATE_____ TIME_____

LOC_____ Rm. _____

MTG TITLE / TOPIC _____

YOUR ROLE _____

ITEMS TO REPORT

▶ _____

▶ _____

▶ _____

▶ _____

▶ _____

Don't forget support documentation!

MISC DETAILS

_____

_____

_____

_____

_____

_____

_____

_____

_____

BRIEFING SLIDES

REQ? ☐ WHEN DUE_____ SUBMIT? ☐ NO. SLIDES ____

MTG NOTES

_____

_____

_____

_____

_____

_____

_____

_____

_____

_____

_____

_____

TASKERS & FOLLOW-UPS – Checkmark your Priorities

☐ _____

POC _____ DUE _____

☐ _____

POC _____ DUE _____

☐ _____

POC _____ DUE _____

☐ _____

POC _____ DUE _____

☐ _____

POC _____ DUE _____

ENTRY 095

DATE_____ TIME_____

LOC_____ Rm. _____

MTG TITLE / TOPIC _____

YOUR ROLE _____

ITEMS TO REPORT

▶ _____

▶ _____

▶ _____

▶ _____

▶ _____

Don't forget support documentation!

MISC DETAILS

_____

_____

_____

_____

_____

_____

_____

_____

_____

BRIEFING SLIDES

REQ? ☐ WHEN DUE _____ SUBMIT? ☐ NO. SLIDES _____

MTG NOTES

_____

_____

_____

_____

_____

_____

_____

_____

_____

_____

_____

_____

TASKERS & FOLLOW-UPS - Checkmark your Priorities

☐ _____

POC _____ DUE _____

☐ _____

POC _____ DUE _____

☐ _____

POC _____ DUE _____

☐ _____

POC _____ DUE _____

☐ _____

POC _____ DUE _____

DATE_____ TIME_____

LOC_____ Rm. _____

MTG TITLE / TOPIC_____

YOUR ROLE _____

ITEMS TO REPORT

▶_____

▶_____

▶_____

▶_____

▶_____

Don't forget support documentation!

MISC DETAILS

_____

_____

_____

_____

_____

_____

_____

_____

_____

BRIEFING SLIDES

REQ? ☐ **WHEN DUE**_____ **SUBMIT?** ☐ **NO. SLIDES** ____

U.S. ARMED FORCES

MTG NOTES

_____

_____

_____

_____

_____

_____

_____

_____

_____

_____

_____

_____

_____

TASKERS & FOLLOW-UPS - Checkmark your Priorities

☐ _____

   POC _____ DUE _____

☐ _____

   POC _____ DUE _____

☐ _____

   POC _____ DUE _____

☐ _____

   POC _____ DUE _____

☐ _____

   POC _____ DUE _____

DATE_____ TIME_____

LOC_____ Rm. _____

MTG TITLE / TOPIC _____

YOUR ROLE _____

ITEMS TO REPORT

▶ _____

▶ _____

▶ _____

▶ _____

▶ _____

Don't forget support documentation!

MISC DETAILS

_____

_____

_____

_____

_____

_____

_____

_____

_____

_____

BRIEFING SLIDES
REQ? ☐ WHEN DUE_____ SUBMIT?☐ NO. SLIDES____

MTG NOTES

_____
_____
_____
_____
_____
_____
_____
_____
_____
_____
_____
_____

TASKERS & FOLLOW-UPS – Checkmark your Priorities

☐ _____

POC _____ DUE _____

☐ _____

POC _____ DUE _____

☐ _____

POC _____ DUE _____

☐ _____

POC _____ DUE _____

☐ _____

POC _____ DUE _____

ENTRY 098

DATE_____ TIME_____

LOC_____ Rm. _____

MTG TITLE / TOPIC _____

YOUR ROLE _____

ITEMS TO REPORT

▶ _____

▶ _____

▶ _____

▶ _____

▶ _____

Don't forget support documentation!

MISC DETAILS

_____

_____

_____

_____

_____

_____

_____

_____

_____

BRIEFING SLIDES

REQ? ☐ WHEN DUE _____ SUBMIT? ☐ NO. SLIDES _____

U.S. ARMED FORCES

MTG NOTES

_____

_____

_____

_____

_____

_____

_____

_____

_____

_____

_____

_____

TASKERS & FOLLOW-UPS – Checkmark your Priorities

☐ _____

   POC _____ DUE _____

☐ _____

   POC _____ DUE _____

☐ _____

   POC _____ DUE _____

☐ _____

   POC _____ DUE _____

☐ _____

   POC _____ DUE _____

ENTRY 099

DATE_____ TIME_____

LOC_____ Rm. _____

MTG TITLE / TOPIC _____

YOUR ROLE _____

ITEMS TO REPORT

▶ _____

▶ _____

▶ _____

▶ _____

▶ _____

Don't forget support documentation!

MISC DETAILS

_____

_____

_____

_____

_____

_____

_____

_____

_____

_____

BRIEFING SLIDES

REQ? ☐ WHEN DUE_____ SUBMIT? ☐ NO. SLIDES _____

MTG NOTES

_____

_____

_____

_____

_____

_____

_____

_____

_____

_____

_____

_____

TASKERS & FOLLOW-UPS – Checkmark your Priorities

☐ _____

POC _____ DUE _____

☐ _____

POC _____ DUE _____

☐ _____

POC _____ DUE _____

☐ _____

POC _____ DUE _____

☐ _____

POC _____ DUE _____

ENTRY 100

DATE_____ TIME_____

LOC_____ Rm. _____

MTG TITLE / TOPIC_____

YOUR ROLE _____

ITEMS TO REPORT

▶ _____

▶ _____

▶ _____

▶ _____

▶ _____

Don't forget support documentation!

MISC DETAILS

_____

_____

_____

_____

_____

_____

_____

_____

_____

BRIEFING SLIDES

REQ? ☐ WHEN DUE_____ SUBMIT? ☐ NO. SLIDES _____

MTG NOTES

_____

_____

_____

_____

_____

_____

_____

_____

_____

_____

_____

_____

_____

TASKERS & FOLLOW-UPS – Checkmark your Priorities

☐ _____

   POC _____ DUE _____

☐ _____

   POC _____ DUE _____

☐ _____

   POC _____ DUE _____

☐ _____

   POC _____ DUE _____

☐ _____

   POC _____ DUE _____

COMING SOON from Yankee Bugle

Deployment Journal - Keep the difficult events of forward deploying in perspective by tracking daily events, the feelings you experience, and offering yourself the ability to review past events with a broad perspective so you can remain emotionally healthy and resilient.
- 120, 180 and 365-day volumes!

PTSD Recovery Journal - Like the deployment journal, putting difficult emotions and experiences into perspective goes a long way toward emotionally handling and coping with traumatic events. Supplement your journey toward a better life by answering simple questions that unlock your mind from unhealthy cycles of thought and belief.

Fitness Tracking Log - Carry on the Yankee Bugle tradition and track your fitness easily with preset areas to create focus areas and track your progress.

Letters to Daddy/Mommy - Are you or your spouse deploying? Select the appropriate book for your child so they can write letters every day to their service member, creating an outlet for frustration, sharing of joys, and a great writing-exercise tool!

U.S. ARMED FORCES